MY
STORY
GOD'S
GLORY

BY

Martina Oluwabunmi Yemi–Akala

First Printing: 2018

ISBN-9781980829744

DEDICATION

This book is dedicated to my parents, Mr. Raphael Aluko and Mrs. Lucy Aluko for your sacrifice of love. Thank you for instilling Godly and sound moral values into me and my siblings. I could not have asked for better role models.

CONTENTS

ACKNOWLEDGEMENT

I appreciate my family, my husband Adeyemi and my children, Heritage and Anointed for their unrelenting support and encouragement. This book would not have been completed and published without them.

My profound gratitude goes to everyone that contributed to the success of this book by devoting time to proofread, edit and design.

To all the special people, my destiny helpers that have been part of my story, the pages of this book are not enough to list names, I am extremely thankful to you all for being there all the way.

INTRODUCTION

"I will sing of the mercies of the Lord forever: with my mouth will I make known Your faithfulness to all generations" Psalms 89:1

I testify that it has been God all the way in my journey of life these decades.

In utmost amazement I listened to my mother narrate the story of my birth some years back and I knew I was not an accident!

From the very beginning of my conception till now, I have been living by God's miracle. Some years ago, on the street of Tooting Broadway in London my mother was walking with so much burden that caused her soul to be downcast. Unknown to her that day her change would come and her burden would be lifted. By divine arrangement she ran into a Christian Priest that came as a missionary to her home town some years back in Nigeria, Africa. The Priest recognised her and called out her name, he said "Lucy you look so sorrowful, it's very unlike the lady I knew in Africa, what is the problem?"

My mother narrated how long she had been waiting to be conceived of a child and all efforts were fruitless. The Priest asked her to kneel down right there on the street and he prayed for her! That same month, my mother conceived and here l am. What a miracle!

Ever since then it has been miracles upon miracles, to God alone be the glory!

My prayer is that as you read the account of my encounter with God, the Creator of the Universe as set out in this book (which in itself is a miracle), your faith will arise and you too can believe God for miracles in your life.

The Bible says in Romans 2:11 *"For there is no partiality with God"*. If God did it for me He can and He will do it for you.

CHAPTER ONE

The greatest miracle of all

"For by grace you have been saved through faith, and that not of ourselves; it is the gift of God, not of works, lest anyone should boast" Ephesians 2:8-9

I grew up normally as every normal girl in a middle class family, daddy working as an accountant, dedicated to work, a man of impeccable integrity and mum was a midwife nurse. My parents taught us the way of the Lord and instilled into us every good moral and conduct you can imagine on this planet. I am grateful to them both. My parents are both now retired enjoying the fruits of their good labours. I pray they continue to enjoy every bit of it in good health in Jesus' name. Amen.

Two things are non-negotiable in my family - solid Christian foundation and sound educational achievements. After my high school, I went to the Federal University of Technology, Akure in Nigeria (Africa) to study Meteorology and obtained a Bachelor's and a Masters' degree in Meteorology. As wonderful as these achievements were, I got something more than a prestigious degree any world Class University can offer.

In January 1991 in my final year I found myself in the Charismatic Student Fellowship after several invitations. I was a Catholic, never missed Mass, going through the motion of religion until this faithful day. The word of God came to me and exposed me to how God sees me, then, I realised all my self-righteousness were like filthy rags before the Creator of the Universe. I was broken and desperately in need of help, Jesus gave me an invitation to come to Him, forgave my sins, cleansed me from all my unrighteousness and made me a child of God.

My life made a 360 degree turn and truly Jesus touched me and I became new, born again- 2 Corinthians 5:17 says *"Therefore if any man be in Christ Jesus, he is a new creation, old things have passed away, behold all things have become new"*

Not only was I a changed person spiritually, my passions, desires, music, dressing, my focus, my company and friends, everything about me changed. I became hungry for God, in His Word and His Presence. Jesus gave my life a meaning, I tasted the sweetness of God's unconditional love as Jesus took all my sins away and filled me with the joy of salvation.

This is the greatest of all the miracles, because God's gift of salvation to me is a total package, consisting of everything I need to live a good life here on earth and reign with Him in eternity.

I don't know where you are in your journey

with life's twists and turns, but I am convinced that life is more than working, paying the bills, going on holiday and acquiring possessions. We are made for a purpose and you can only discover this by connecting to the One that created you. The manufacturer decides the use and purpose of his invention. Give your heart to Jesus and let Him give your life a meaning.

God of Impossibilities

Man, as knowledgeable as he is, still has limits and incapable of doing many things; only God can do that which no man can do.

There are times in life when things are hard and we are pressed on all sides it looks like there is no way out; what do we do? Who do we turn to? As children of God, saved and redeemed, we are not exempt from challenges and difficult times, but the joyful assurance is that we are never alone.

The Bible in Isaiah 43: 1 -2 says *"But now thus says the Lord who created you, O Jacob, and He who formed you, O Israel. Fear not, for I have redeemed you; I have called you by your name, You are Mine. When you pass through the waters, I will be with you and through the rivers, they shall not overflow you. When you walk through the fire you shall not be burned, nor the flame scorch you"*

Waters, rivers and fire are metaphoric and symbolise overwhelming challenges and trials of our faith. Such times only come to make us strong and bring glory unto God as He takes us through.

I entered into the University in 1986 for a five year course. During my under graduate days, the first 2 Years were very difficult and I struggled with some of my courses, I had to re-sit a few and carry over some. Those two years were a mess and I was trailing behind most of my course mates.

Until one day, it dawned on me that if something drastic did not happen to me I will spend more years than required and graduate eventually without a decent degree. So I began to strategize and project how many courses I needed to do and the grades I needed to achieve the required Cumulate Grade Points (CGP).

In order to ease off the load, I focused only on the main courses and left out the 'electives'. By the time I was in year 4, I had stabilised and had my eyes set on graduating the following year.

At the end of second semester in the final year, I was summoned into the Departmental office and I was told that I had not completed the required units of the compulsory electives and so will not graduate that year and I had to spend an extra year in the university to complete the outstanding electives.

My world quickly collapsed underneath me, the thought of not graduating with my mates was very demoralising and I wept and wept for days. My parents were deeply disappointed but thank God for the brothers and sisters in Church and friends who kept encouraging and upholding me in prayers.

One day, one of my friends visited me at home and suggested how to reduce the extra one year to one semester. As good as that sounded then, it looked highly impossible because two of the courses were in the second semester and one in first, so a whole year was guaranteed.

One of the two courses was administered by another department (Geophysics department) and the other by my department. So my friend suggested that we approach the head of Geophysics department to see if he would allow me to enrol for the course in first semester, just me and of course run the course still at the usual time. We both did not know what the outcome will be.

To our greatest amazement, he agreed! Oh my joy knew no bounds, it is a miracle. With this result, of course, my own department had no choice but to run the course in the first semester too! Nothing is impossible with God. The Lord did what has never been done in the history of both departments. He suspended all policies and protocols just for my sake. God makes impossibilities possible, He makes a way where there is no way.

I don't know what seems impossible in your life, the mighty hand of God can turn things around for your good. What God did for me was like a dream, truly according to the Holy Scriptures in Psalm 126:1

"When the Lord turned again the captivity of Zion we were like them that dreamt"

Whatever the problem, call on Him and He will show up. Jesus calmed the raging storm of the sea when He was in the boat with the disciples, call on His name, His name is Miracle.

CHAPTER 2

God is never late

" But do not forget this one thing, dear
friends, with the Lord a day is like a thousand
years and a thousand years are like a day" 2
Peter 3:8

Delay is not denial, and though it feels
and looks like answers to prayers are
delayed, promises seem unfulfilled, you
must know that God is coming and He is coming
big. God make things beautiful in His own time.

There is a touch of impatience in every one of
us and one of the difficult things in life is
waiting for anything! We live in an era where
almost everything happens virtually instantly,
family meals made ready within 5 minutes,

where already processed food can just be heated up in microwaves speedily. The effort of cooking from scratch and the time of waiting for the cooked food has been eradicated. We hate any delays whatsoever, in fact we submit claims to organisations (e.g. transport companies) for compensation in any delays caused to our journeys.

Waiting for things is never pleasant and the same goes when we wait on the Lord for the fulfilment of His promises, the waiting is never easy but when the desire comes, it is always like a tree of life. Proverbs 13:12

God's promises to His children are priceless, nothing compares and they are worth waiting for. The longer the wait, most of the time, the more glorious the package. God promised Abraham a child and he waited 25 years. Waiting demands patience, endurance and faith, knowing that He that promised is not a man and He will not fail on His promises.

Numbers 23:19

"God is not a man that He should lie, nor a son of man that He should repent. Has He said, and will not do? Or has He spoken, and will He not make it good?"

When we wait for God's promises, our waiting is never in vain, because we believe that faithful is He that promised and He will do it! While we wait in earnest expectations we have set times and how the promises should be fulfilled, we even go ahead to rehearse how we will stand before the congregation of God to testify of His faithfulness, God is a Father that delivers on His promises.

God's timing – The best

"He has made everything beautiful in His time. Also He has put eternity in their hearts, except that no one can find out the work that God does from beginning to end" Ecclesiastes 3:11

When I graduated from the University, the Lord gave me a fantastic job and my career kicked off with a great future ahead of me. As things started to look good the expectation to be married set in: parents, relatives, neighbours and all well-wishers were full of expectations. For parents after graduation from the University, the next cause for celebration is wedding! Two years into my job, loved ones started asking questions.

My parents were particularly concerned especially when "marriageable men" kept coming and I didn't accept any of their proposals. They were mostly believers from other Churches but the Lord had spoken to me long before then that my husband was in my Ministry, Charismatic Renewal Ministries (CRM) and that He will give me a lovely home. This promise of God was my anchor and guide, it removed every form of confusion.

When the pressure was on, I continued to serve God and just like Zachariah and Elizabeth, God brought my miracle to the place of my assignment. **The place of service is the place of divine visitation.**

Zacharias and Elizabeth were at their place of assignment (temple) serving the Lord for years occupying as a priest waiting for the promise of God. The Lord met them and rewarded them with the blessing of John the Baptist, and of all the men born by a woman none can be compared unto him (Luke 2:5-14)

On this fateful day, I went to visit the choir in one of our Church branches in another town and that same day I met this brother in Christ who travelled from another city for a job assignment in that neighbourhood and that was it, today the same man is my husband.

How we met was a divine arrangement considering where we were both located in the country, God is a Rewarder. Although in the eyes of men it looked like time was running out, God did it at His own beautiful time.

While we wait for the miracle, the breakthrough, we must be fervent in serving the Lord. By the grace of God our marriage is 21 years and it's been a wonderful journey simply because whatever God does is always perfect.

Wait for the Lord, He is never late. Don't try to help God, don't just settle for anything, God has the best for you, His plan for us is good and never evil (Jeremiah 29:11)

The question is, what do we do while waiting,

so that we don't give up before we receive the promises?

Manage all expectations to your advantage: Once you are assured of God's love for you and you have understanding of His plan then anything said by anyone contrary to this should be repudiated.

In life we don't have control over what people say to us but we have absolute control over how we allow what is said to affect us, we can interpret negative words positively so that it lifts us rather than pull us down.

Remain at the place of assignment: The devil finds work for idle hands, don't be idle, get busy, serving God with all your heart. When you are busy working for the Lord, there is little or no room for the enemy to torment you with what you should have and don't have. God is too righteous to forget your labour of love.

<u>Don't try to help God:</u> There is the tendency to seek for an alternative to God, to have a plan B so as not to place all your eggs in one basket. As a child of God, if God does not help you, you cannot be helped! This is because our help only comes from Him when we look to him. Trusting in man is vain because man is limited but the Almighty God is the One that is unlimited in power, unlimited in resources, unlimited in grace.

Sarah, Abraham's wife tried to help God because she had waited for the promise of a child and it looked like the promise was never going to come because both herself and her husband were far beyond child bearing age but God fulfilled His promise and Isaac the covenant son was born. (Genesis 16)

<u>Have faith and don't doubt:</u> We must never doubt the ability of God to do what He says He will do. When we doubt God, we are in effect questioning His integrity and ability. God is able

to do far more than we expect (Ephesians 3:20). God rewards those that believe that He is!

Doubt shifts our focus from God. We can trust God because He never fails: He has never failed and He will never fail. The world may fail, friends may betray, families may disappoint, but God never fails.

Be patient, God's timing is the best: Patience is a virtue and it has a role to play in preparing us for the blessings ahead. The waiting time is a time to develop spiritually, physically, mentally and emotionally.

Understand that life is in seasons: Life is in seasons and the seasons differ from one person to another. That is why you cannot compare yourself to someone else. This understanding helps us to make the most of every season. If you are in the season of sowing don't start wishing to be in harvest season. Sowing time comes before harvest time.

Ecclesiastes 3:1 *"To everything there is a season, a time for every purpose under heaven"*
Gen 8:22 *"While the earth remains, Seedtime and harvest, Cold and heat. Winter and summer and day and night shall not cease"*

One season must come before the next one can come so enjoy every blessing that comes with each season.

Winter may not be as exciting as summer but while we look forward to summer, enjoy the uniqueness of winter- Snow is beautiful to behold.

Don't doubt, have faith

God promised my husband and I a lovely home with our children surrounding our table like olive branches and so we were so sure that we would have our own children in no time.

Traditionally in the culture where I grew up, it is almost impossible to be married and opt not to have children as a personal choice. By the first anniversary of wedding, child dedication is usually expected. Holding onto God's promises which include His Godly seed, we hoped for children of our own.

My husband and I are Children Evangelists and we are both passionate about children and committed to teaching them to know God at a very young age and becoming committed followers of Jesus Christ. Our desire to have our own grew daily as we see God do amazing things through young children He placed under our care.

We kept hoping and expecting God's visitation like He visited Zachariah and Elizabeth. Year in year out, for seven years! It was an experience. I learnt life lessons, and one of these is how to wait on the Lord.

In the cause of waiting, many advisors and counsellors came around, of course they were genuinely concerned. A family member once said to my husband that when people have a challenge of childlessness like ours, the Bible is not enough!

We know that the promises of God are yea and amen! Every good and perfect gift comes from God (James 1:17)

My husband told the family member, we were not going to help God, we have no alternative plan, and it is either God blesses us or God blesses us. In demonstrating our faith in the Lord, we kept buying cloths for our future children knowing that the expectations of the righteous cannot be cut off.

On two different occasions, I became pregnant, the first time it was the confirmation we needed that nothing was wrong medically with us, although it was painful that the joy was momentary, we encouraged ourselves that God will and can do it again.

Few years later, I was pregnant again and this time I was carrying twins!!! You cannot imagine how much joy filled our hearts. In no time, my physical appearance changed and it became obvious to people around that I had conceived. Friends, family, everyone were over the moon with joy but this was unexpectedly short lived too, as one after the other I lost both babies.

I was devastated and my pain was exceedingly overwhelming, I cried inconsolably. My husband had to stay strong to comfort me even though he was equally hurting.

Truly many are the afflictions of the righteous but God delivers him from them all (Psalm 34:19)

God knows the end from the beginning

After the loss of the second pregnancy the Lord spoke to us, He told us to get ready to relocate to the United Kingdom (UK) to support the work of the ministry there and that He will make the place our land of refuge and bless us with our own children.

It was a great struggle because shortly before then my husband got a job with Shell Petroleum after a long time of waiting to be employed. We heard God clearly and not yielding was not an option. God also spoke to a few of our Church family and friends diversely.

While we were still pondering on how this will play out, one of my husband's colleagues showed up at the house and said God told him there is a project we were going to embark on and he wanted to be a part of it. He gave us money and when we counted, it was what was needed to purchase the ticket. God is truly the Jehovah Jireh the God our Provider.

The Lord perfected everything and not long my husband and I relocated to the UK. We were consumed with the thoughts of finding our feet, understanding the system and settling as the case may be when one relocates to a new place, different culture, everything was a shock to our system but God came ahead of us. He planted His children, brothers and sisters in Christ on our pathway who were of great help to us.

True to God's promises, I became pregnant again!!! I was taunted with my past experiences but the Lord God saw me through. Our lovely daughter, God's Heritage was born!!! Jubilation heralded all over the world. A dream come true, a desire granted, the long awaited blessing came finally. Rejoicing, dancing and gladness galore!

We became parents, father and mother of a miracle and the most beautiful baby in our eyes. It's such a joy that you don't even want to recover from.

My husband and I had not recovered from the joy of the gift of God to us while I discovered I was pregnant again and God's Anointed came in grand style defying all medical presumptions.

God has the final say

Thirty two weeks into our first daughter's pregnancy, I had a very severe pre-eclampsia that resulted in God's Heritage being born 5 weeks earlier and so the doctor said my subsequent pregnancies will not grow to full term because of my past. Immediately, the word of God came to my mind –

Lamentation 3:37
"Who is he who speaks and it comes to pass when the Lord has not commanded it?"

Our second child was full term, she was not in a haste at all, and she came at God's appointed time. In the space of two years God blessed us with two children! When God opens a door, no man can shut it.

We are so satisfied with the two children God blessed us with. Friend, who would have thought a time will come when we would say, "we've had enough" As I ponder on things, I came to understand why God allowed the previous losses. He knows the end from the beginning, all along God was preserving my life, I may not have survived the complications I had during God's Heritage's pregnancy if I was not in the UK at the time. All things work all together for good to them that love God.

CHAPTER 3

God is a Healer

My childhood was typified with a lot of visits to the hospital as I was constantly ill that my parents were unsure if I was going to survive. In my elementary school days, I was rushed to the hospital where my mum worked on many occasions, and it kept going on and on until my undergraduate days when I met the Lord Who touched me, healed me and made me whole!

From that time I started to enjoy His divine health and I became free from all the repeated medical prescriptions that I was hooked on. After I got married, I started experiencing difficulty in breathing and the doctor said I was asthmatic. It grew worse and I was placed on medication again. The doctor made me to realise that there is no medical cure for this type of ailment and that he will support me to manage the development, but I knew all I needed was a MIRACLE.

My day of visitation

A prayer like "May you never miss your day of visitation is not cliché"

In 1999, a 7-Day prayer and fasting programme was organised and everyone in Church was expected to participate unless you had medical reasons or other valid reasons not to.

Every evening we all met together at the church venue to pray. The first day of the programme went well and I felt spiritually refreshed and the second day, the asthma attack struck with terrible agonizing pain that left me struggling to breathe and I felt my diaphragm closing up so tightly. My rib bones were extremely painful and I knew I had to take my medication instantly.

As I got up to pick the medicine, I heard the

Lord say **"don't"** so I left the medicine and I was wondering what next because I was in so much pain that I just wanted to break the fast by taking my medicine and concluded that God will understand. I stood up again to get it and again loud and clear I heard His voice saying **"don't"** and I broke down in tears uncontrollably. I was alone at home so I decided to go out from the house away from the medicine for a long walk just to avoid falling into the temptation of going against the instruction of God.

It was drawing near to the time of prayer and all I kept praying for was for God to help me till I get to Church. In my mind that would be a perfect place for me to pass out and the prayer of God's children can revive me and if not, I would go to be with Jesus in heaven.

Thinking back at that time, I was definitely not afraid of death, I'm still not afraid because my eternity is sealed in Christ Jesus! If you are afraid to die, you need Jesus. He is the One that conquered death and gave us victory over death. He came to give life and to give it more abundantly. Anyone that believes in Him will never perish but have eternal life.

The Bible says in 1 Corinthians 15: 50-57

"Now this I say, brethren, that flesh and blood cannot inherit the kingdom of God; nor does corruption inherit incorruption. Behold, I tell you a mystery: We shall not all sleep, but we shall all be changed— in a moment, in the twinkling of an eye, at the last trumpet. For the trumpet will sound, and the dead will be raised incorruptible, and we shall be changed. For this corruptible must put on incorruption, and this mortal must put on immortality. So when this corruptible has put on incorruption, and this mortal has put on immortality, then shall be brought to pass the saying that is written:

"Death is swallowed up in victory."
"O Death, where is your sting?
O Hades, where is your victory?"

The sting of death is sin, and the strength of sin is the law.
But thanks be to God, who gives us the victory through our
Lord Jesus Christ"

Well, the Lord did the miraculous in my life that day. While people were praising God in the Church I was struggling hard due to pain but as I focused on God, all of a sudden, the pain in my ribs left. I was so relieved and then I felt my lungs opening up and words started coming out slowly from my mouth. Surely this was a miracle as I started to sing softly at the start and before the end of the praise session, I could sing fluently without any pain. In astonishment of what God did in my life, I began to sing so loudly to celebrate the miracle of healing. Jesus touched me and made me whole. To the glory of God, that was the end of the ailment that the doctor said was incurable.

Jesus is still healing the sick, giving sight to the blind, making the barren to keep house and raising the dead. Hallelujah!

The Power of praise

"Whosoever offers praise glorifies God" Psalm 50:23

There is power in praise! When we praise God, He steps into our situations and takes over completely that we would have no need to do a thing. He confronts our oppressors, fights our battles until our enemies are defeated.

In 2 Chronicles 20-23 when the people of Ammon and Moab came against Judah in battle, the Lord told Jehoshaphat to prepare singers who will sing praises and their enemies fought themselves until they destroyed themselves.

21 And when he had consulted with the people, he appointed those who should sing to the Lord, and who should praise the beauty of holiness, as they went out before the army and were saying: "Praise the Lord, for His mercy endures forever." 22 Now when they began to sing and to praise, the Lord set ambushes against the people of Ammon, Moab, and Mount Seir, who had come against Judah; and they were defeated.

23 For the people of Ammon and Moab stood up against the inhabitants of Mount Seir to utterly kill and destroy them. And when they had made an end of the inhabitants of Seir, they helped to destroy one another.

In Acts chapter 16, during a session of praise and prayer led by Paul and Silas while in the prison (they were imprisoned for healing a slave girl who had an unclean spirit).God came down and by His power, the chains with which they were bound shattered and the secured doors flung open of their own accord.

Praise moves the hands of God in our favour, in challenging and difficult times. I have learnt to praise the One Who is worthy to be praised and I have been saved from my afflictions.

CHAPTER 4

God in good and bad times

Isaiah 43:2
When you pass through the waters, I will be
with you;
And through the rivers, they shall not overflow
you.
When you walk through the fire, you shall not
be burned,
nor shall the flame scorch you.

Bad things happen to good people sometimes and it is not always because they have sinned, Job was a classic example. The life of a believer is not void of difficult times but even in such a situation God never leaves us without help.

One of the most difficult times in my life was the time my brother unexpectedly went to be with the Lord. The loss of a loved one is ever so grievous and it does not matter whether such a person is young or old, although admittedly, the death of a young one hits terribly bad and the pain goes so deep.

The cloud of sorrow that engulfed my family was indescribable. My husband and I suddenly stepped into the role of the eldest carrying the heavy burden on our shoulders. Both my parents were broken beyond imagination.

Their devastation hit me even more than the death of my brother and I desperately wanted to make their pains go away.

If you are a parent and you are reading this book, I pray that you will never experience sorrow over any of your children. Your joy will not be cut short and your labour over your children will never be in vain in Jesus' name. Amen.

My brother of blessed memory was the first believer in the family, fervent in serving the Lord and so I couldn't understand why he would die at such an unripe age.

It dawned on me very quickly that it is only by the mercies of God that we have not been consumed because His compassion never fails (Lamentation 3:22).

What will I be remembered for?

Death is a debt owed by all. A colleague of mine said to me some years ago that there are three realities of life,
1) You are born,
2) You die and
3) You pay taxes

It's a thin line between life and death and we must learn to value and enjoy our lives and more importantly leave a godly legacy behind.

It is not how long necessarily but how impactful. However, it is God's plan that His children live long and fulfil purpose. No one is here by accident or to make up the number, God has a purpose for everyone, we just need to discover it!

If you have been wondering what your purpose in life is, why not ask your Creator? He is the Potter and we are the clay. He decides what the vessel is to be used for and anything outside of this leads to frustration, lack of fulfilment and unfruitfulness.

I asked myself, when I am no more, what will I be remembered for, how many people would I have touched with the love of God and His kindness.

Life is only worth living when there is something to live for.

God my Comforter

Weeks after my brother passed on, I finally got my opportunity to grieve. I was no longer playing the role of the super woman that must be strong for everyone. I was finally all alone most of the time.

In the lowest time of our lives we understand how valuable people are. It was great having friends and members of the Church around to comfort me, this notwithstanding, in my lonely moments, the only One that was always present to comfort me was the Holy Spirit my Comforter, sweet Holy Spirit.

One day in my pool of tears, God said to me **"He took him away from the evil which was to come"**.

He brought me through that difficult time, I don't know how, but He did it. Each day, He lightened the pain, He gave me beauty for ashes and the oil of joy for mourning!

God held me and the family firmly and brought us to the other side of victory.

God my Helper

No earthly father will abandon their children in times of difficulty or in pain. Why do we think our heavenly Father will be insensitive to our grief or care less when we are in despair?

We have a high Priest Who is touched by our feelings, Jesus Christ our Saviour, so He cannot ignore our pains. He understands. (Hebrew 4:15)

Today, many people have turned their backs on God because they blamed Him for the loss of a dear one. They question and doubt His existence because He did not prevent the calamity that struck. God alone knows the end from the beginning and He remains Unquestionable.

In our difficult times, He is reaching out to help, comfort, heal our wounds and make us whole again. The strategy of the devil is to isolate us from where our help is, don't give in to the evil one and don't give up on God, help is on the way. God is our ever-present help in times of troubles.

Many are the afflictions of the righteous (yes the righteous can be afflicted and troubled!) but God delivers him from them all (Psalms 34:19). When we allow God to help us through our difficult times, everything we experienced then becomes a life saver for another.

In difficult times many look for a way out of the pain and grief by retrieving into themselves and taking drastic steps that are harmful, I found relief in talking to good people, my church network and friends, who sometimes just took time to listen to me or just sit quietly, all these helped me through the challenging time.

A problem shared is a problem half solved.

Bottled up grieve could degenerate to all sorts of health issues, so seek for help.

There cannot be testimonies without tests, God wants to turn whatever mess we find ourselves into messages, our trials into triumph and ultimately our story gives Him glory.

CHAPTER 5

God my Promise Keeper

For exaltation *comes* neither from the east
Nor from the west nor from the south.
But God *is* the Judge:
He puts down one,
And exalts another. Psalm 75:6-7

I am a woman helped by God! I relocated to the UK holding onto nothing but God's promises and the assurance of His faithfulness.

I was certain that whatever I will become in the UK can never be outside of God's help and intervention and so I started hunting for jobs but very conscious of God's instructions to me and so my pursuit was primarily a job that will be flexible and not infringe on my availability for the work of God and my family.

My desperation to be employed was driven by the fact that it is one of the requirements set by UK Immigration for citizens who plan to invite their spouse for permanent residency in the UK.

My CV was sent to different organisations of interest far and wide and I submitted tons of applications also, but to my disappointment all came back with unfavourable responses such as: "you do not have the experience or skill for the role"

My little beginning

Not too long I got a job at McDonald's Restaurant through the help of my host. I remember calling my husband with so much excitement sharing my news. I didn't know what to expect but I was just glad I got a job!

My first day was a complete disaster! I turned up and I was paired with another staff working at the drive-through section, apparently he was supposed to teach me the trade. It didn't take my trainer long to discover that I didn't know the currency denominations and all of that.

He alerted the team leader and I was quickly moved to another assignment - clearing the tables, emptying the bins, cleaning the surroundings and the toilets.

Although my shift was not a full day shift, I was so shattered that I didn't look forward to returning to work the following day.

I continued for three weeks and one day I came to my senses and I asked myself "what am I doing here". There was no resemblance at all of where I was with the vision that God showed me about my future in the land He relocated me to and I intensified my search for jobs and cried out to God to get me out of McDonald's!

I needed a stable job with regular income to be able to invite my husband, and the desire was for us to settle in the land within seven months of my arrival.

By the second month my husband was already expecting a concrete arrangement towards his coming. My next job was the role of a receptionist with Group 4 Securitas. It was regular and there was no requirement to work weekends. So I accepted the job offer.

I was based at the Benefit Agency office and in addition to my reception duties, I provided security at the waiting area where claimants wait to receive their benefits. It became obvious very quickly that I was only just passing through the job, it was nothing like what the Lord showed me.

My company issued us with uniforms and so it was easy to identify us as 'officers in charge' The job was very challenging and I knew I needed more than physical authority to maintain order; I needed spiritual authority to take charge. Through this experience I learnt patience, endurance and longsuffering. I knew the job would help me to meet the requirements of inviting my husband, which includes getting an accommodation and having sufficient funds: evidence that I can take care of my husband when he arrives in the UK. So I held on to it.

God of wonders

Plans to invite my husband started as soon as the immigration requirements were met and I travelled to Nigeria to attend the interview with him at the British High Commission. To God be the praise, the interview went well and he was given his visa immediately. We travelled together back into the UK in October 2001 I was overwhelmed with joy because I had resolved not to return to the UK alone!

My husband and I started working together regarding our future in the UK, he started looking for a job and I continued with my search for another. One of my friends worked in the Job Centre office, so she always sent application jobs across my way.

I had my eyes set on joining the Civil Service for a lot of reasons. There were three government

Departments where I was working as a receptionist and there were vacancies in one of the department for the role of Administrative Officers and I applied, the role was for 9 months. I got the job and for the first time I was in an environment that looked like what God showed me.

The role was an interesting one and nine months flew by quickly and I was a job seeker again. I was confident that there will be an opening in another government department.

Shortly before my contract at my place of work elapsed, I had an interview in one of the Local Authorities and on my way God drew my attention to a 15 storey building and **He said "this is where you will work"**

I had no clue which organisation occupied the building nor any idea of what they did at that time. I later received an application form from my friend and the vacancy was in the building that the Lord drew my attention to. Awesome!

God said so!

I was shortlisted and invited to attend an interview. By this time, I was noticeably pregnant with my second child and my colleague who also applied and didn't get an interview mocked and said "as soon as they set their eyes on you they will find a reason not to give you the job. Who wants to give a pregnant woman a job knowing she will soon disappear on maternity holiday"

To God be the glory, I got the job! I got a job in the building God told me and I have been with the organisation 13 years now; it has been one good story after the other.

I joined the organisation when they were merging with another government department although my role was meant to be a permanent role, the uncertainties around the merging meant I could only the offered a post on a fixed term contract for a period of one year because they were unsure how the restructuring would affect my section.

I accepted the offer and after the 12 weeks training I went to have my baby but returned to work after three months. The restructuring affected so many colleagues and they were without a job, the department had to absorb them into other suitable roles. My case was different as God would have it. After my contract elapsed, it was renewed for three months, and another three months. By this time it had become apparent that the jobs in my section were staying, and more staff were required at different levels to deliver the task.

Most of my colleagues were allowed to apply for promotion but I wasn't because I was on a fixed term contract. I could only reapply for my post on a permanent contract, which I did.

After this promotion exercise, it was as if heaven closed up and there was no opportunity for career progression for another 6 years. I will say this was like a dessert experience but I kept doing my job as unto the Lord trusting that He will turn things around because I understood that the living God that brought me to the organisation is a faithful God.

This was rewarding in a way, I was nominated to attend the Royal Party Garden hosted by Her Majesty the Queen. It was an honour!

Opportunity came knocking

The saying: "Opportunity once missed can never be regained" is so true!

An opportunity for personal development with the option of obtaining a professional qualification that is recognised outside of my organisation came.

I enrolled for the training programme and by God's grace, I completed all the courses, passed the examinations and obtained the professional qualification. Shortly after I completed the programme, there was another restructuring that led to the creation of a highly technical team that required highly skilled tax professionals with tax professional qualifications- the qualification I just obtained!!

When God wants to promote His children, He opens doors of opportunities to prepare them for the next level He is taking them to. I pray that you will never miss such opportunities in life in Jesus name. Amen!

It turned out that the jobs that were advertised were two grades above my grade then and the normal thing at the time was that you move from one grade to the next, a two steps move was alien. I didn't think I could be allowed to apply but the protocols were suspended and I was told that anyone that had the essential requirements which mainly was the tax professional qualification could apply. This was another intervention of God.

So it happened that after the six years of waiting and hoping, I got a double promotion, it was an amazing wonder, it looked impossible but when God says it's your time for blessing nothing can stop it. When you have Christ you have it all. How many times have you been let down by human beings, people that are in a position to help you but didn't?

In the Bible, John 5:1-15 (NKJV), we read the experience of people at the pool of Bethesda. This is the pool where the sick, the blind, the lame gathered hoping for a miraculous healing after an angel of the Lord came to stir the water. The first person that jumped in received the miracle. It was the survival of the fittest.

There was a man who had an illness for 38 years and he missed so many opportunities to be the first to jump into the water because no matter how hard he struggled someone else overtook him and there was no one to help him. What a hindrance, what a disadvantage. Everyone at one point in life will need help, a support, and a comfort. I appreciate families, friends, church families, and colleagues. As much as they willingly want to be there, they cannot be there at all times.

The question I asked is, where is the family of the man at the pool? Why didn't anyone come to help? May be they lived in another country, or were working or just busy with their own issues.

The Help to the helpless – JESUS, showed up one day, and in one day, the illness of 38 years was terminated! One day made a difference in the life of this man and his life was turned around for good. The ancient Protocol of waiting for an angel at a certain time was suspended on his behalf. When Jesus stepped into his life sickness left permanently and he was made whole. Jesus put an end to the misery of 38 years.

I know I need the Divine at all times, the One that is always there – Jesus the Son of God. He is not only available at all times, He can also do anything, He calms the storm, He fed thousands of people from the lunch of a young boy and there were baskets of left overs. He gives sight to the blind and can raise the dead.

You may have been struggling on your own to rise to the top without anyone to help and without much success and it may even look like you are at a disadvantage and there are structural barriers that you cannot cross because of your background, lack of qualification and physical inadequacies etc. today I introduce and connect you to Jesus, the Help of the helpless for your miracle in Jesus' name. Amen.

And again!

As you can imagine, a double promotion made a lot of difference in my career, my finances, and it opened further doors of blessings. While I was still revelling in the joy of my double blessings, God did it again! I got another promotion.

What God promised to do He is doing now and I cannot but testify of all He has done for me these years. His love is indescribable and unquantifiable, that's the reason for this book. Jesus gives my life a meaning and I live for Him Who loves me and demonstrated that love on Calvary by giving His life for me.

CHAPTER 6

Blessed to be a blessing

"Blessed *be* the God and Father of our Lord Jesus Christ, who has blessed us with every spiritual blessing in the heavenly places in Christ" Ephesians 1:3

I cannot finish this book without testifying to God's grace upon my life to enter into purpose in all spheres as a woman saved by grace. Truly every blessing, spiritual and natural has been given us to impact our world. The gift of salvation, the blessing of a good husband, a wonderful home and an amazing career is given to us so that we can live a purposeful life.

As a woman I understand that God's plan is that I fulfil purpose in three major areas: My home, in ministry and in my career. God made a woman to be a suitable, comparable helper for her husband and so a woman has a calling to her husband. There is a saying that beside every successful man, there is a woman! Fulfilling the role of a wife and a mother, building a godly home is already daunting and to combine this with a career and the work of the ministry is not an easy task but all accomplishable by God's grace.

A colleague asked at a time how I spent my weekend and I gave her a download of my activities and she asked "how do you manage". Sincerely, I can't explain because I know it has never been by my power or might but by divine help.

The grace that works

The Bible says in 2 Corinthians 12:9

And He said to me, "My grace is sufficient for you, for My strength is made perfect in weakness." Therefore most gladly I will rather boast in my infirmities, that the power of Christ may rest upon me.

God invited us to the throne of grace where we can obtain mercy and find help for the time of our needs. This grace is the divine enablement that helps us to do what we would ordinarily be incapable of doing.

To build a godly home, to be successful in career and ministry, we need God's grace. God does not want us to be successful at home and be a failure in our career or ministry neither does he want us to be successful in our career or ministry and make a shipwreck of our marriages and home. God's plan is that we succeed in these areas simultaneously. None of these should be slain on the altar of sacrifice for the other.

Every woman needs wisdom to build her own home, that wisdom comes from God and not from 'friends' or colleagues. It is important that we build on a right foundation, not on our cultures and traditions that cannot stand the test of time.

The Bible tells us that the wise man builds upon the rock, when we make Christ the foundation and the centre of our lives, He holds everything together.

I've committed my life and all about me into the hands of the One that has the whole world in His hands and it is by His unfailing grace that I have been able to juggle and balance my role as a wife and a mother, ministry and career.

It is very common to pursue career at the expense of building a home. Another thing that is equally common is to vigorously pursue the work of the ministry and neglect the home, spouse and children.

In recent times the attack on homes is upsetting, and the rate of divorce is worrying. No one can understand what will make a marriage successful than the One that instituted marriage between Adam and Eve in the Garden of Eden. He wants to build our home and make our marriages a bliss here on earth.

That is not to say there won't be challenging times, it only means that when they come, the marriage will stay strong and through it develop stronger bond because it is built on a solid foundation, Jesus Christ.

Our home is our safe haven, communities, nations and the Church stem from homes that is why it is important we get it right at the home front.

I attended a marriage seminar recently and the speaker said marriage is a covenant and not a contract. In a contract all the parties to the contract are in it for what they can get partly or equally depending on the terms of the contract. In a covenant, each party is in it to give all and to serve.

As a career woman and God's servant, I understood that successful career is not in itself the end but a means to the desired end; which is to fulfil our purpose on earth. As we build our career, we must do our work as unto Him, so that in everything we do God is glorified. Let us serve faithfully, when we are faithful in little things God will commit bigger responsibilities into our hands. Serving faithfully in any career requires godly virtues of commitment, hard work, excellence, loyalty, honesty which enables us to demonstrate excellent work culture. By these, Joseph, Jacob, Esther, Deborah, Ruth, Ezra and Daniel were acknowledged and preferred among many as God would always show Himself strong in such lives.

Our gifts and talents must be used to serve God and build His Church because we shall surely give account to the Giver of the gifts how we invested our talents and how much profit is gained from the investment. The account in Matthew 25:14-30 about the parable of the sower showed that the servants that invested their talents and their investments for profit were given more. The unprofitable servant that did nothing with the talents giving to him, what he had was taken away and he suffered eternal punishment.

We are blessed to be a blessing, our world must rejoice that we passed through this planet. I pray that we will put our trust in God, the Giver of grace. My prayer is that God will visit and revive every home that is experiencing turbulence and at the verge of sinking. He is still doing miracles, there is nothing too difficult for Him to do.

Anyone can be blessed and also be a blessing, all such a person needs is to connect to the All Sufficient God.

SUMMARY

From the very first chapter to the end, I have been able to share my testimonies of God's faithfulness in the 50 years He has given me so far to graciously explore the earth. He came through when challenges came to drown me, He established me in a home, made me a wife, a very necessary helper to my beloved husband, mother to God's Heritage and Anointed.

As if that was not enough, He gave me supernatural grace to combine these responsibilities with doing a work as God's servant to people. It didn't just end there, He crowned my efforts with successes and gave me a beautiful career with records of successes and promotions. I stand tall to say God is indeed a faithful God. All has been by His grace for no one can receive anything except it was given from above.

The book of James 1: 17 says
"Whatever is good and perfect is a gift coming down to us from God our Father, who created all the lights in the heaven He never changes or casts a shifting shadow" (*New Living Translation*)

My life is a testimony of God's wonderful blessings! I make bold to tell you that God wants to bless you so that you can be a blessing. The totality of God's blessing is in Christ Jesus, will you accept God's gift?

John3:16 says:
"For God so loved the world that He gave His only begotten Son, that whoever believes in Him should not perish but have everlasting life"

I pray that my story will help you to understand the length, the breath and width of His love for mankind and for you as a person.
God bless

Printed in Poland
by Amazon Fulfillment
Poland Sp. z o.o., Wrocław